Jig and Mag

by Bobby Lynn Maslen
pictures by John R. Maslen

Scholastic Inc.
New York • Toronto • London • Auckland • Sydney • Mexico City • New Delhi • Hong Kong • Buenos Aires

Beginning sounds for Book 7:

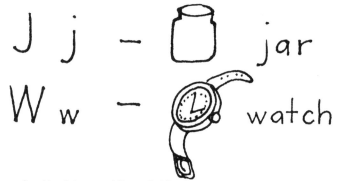

J j – jar
W w – watch

Ask for Bob Books at your local bookstore, or visit www.bobbooks.com.

No part of this publication may be reproduced, stored in a retrieval system, or transmitted in any form or by any means, electronic, mechanical, photocopying, recording, or otherwise, without written permission of the publisher. For information regarding permission, write to Scholastic Inc., Attention: Permissions Department, 557 Broadway, New York, NY 10012.

ISBN 0-439-17551-8

Copyright © 1976 by Bobby Lynn Maslen. All rights reserved. Published by Scholastic Inc. by arrangement with Bob Books ® Publications LLC. SCHOLASTIC and associated logos are trademarks and/or registered trademarks of Scholastic Inc. BOB BOOKS is a registered trademark of Bob Books Publications LLC.

6 5 4 3   6 7 8 9 10 11/0

Printed in China
This edition first printing, May 2006

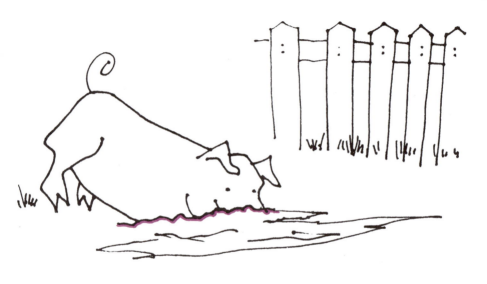

Jig can dig and dig.

Mag can dig and dig.

Did Jig win? Did Mag win?

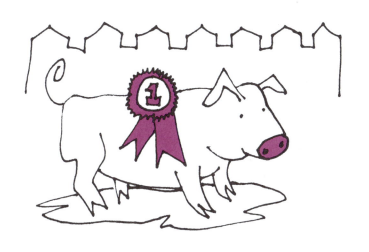

Jig did win.

Jig and Mag ran.

Mag can tag Jig.

Mag did win.

Available Bob Books®:

Set 1: Beginning Readers
Set 2: Advancing Beginners
Set 3: Word Families
Set 4: Compound Words
Set 5: Long Vowels